Our New H

Written by Catherine Mackenzie
Illustrated by Lynn Breeze

Digger the dog is hiding in every picture in this book. Can you find him?

My name is Katie. This is my mum and dad, my friend Max and Digger the dog. My family is moving house. I am sad that we are leaving. Dad says, 'Thank God for all the good things you can see. Then you won't be sad.

Max helps me pack my toys into a box. 'You have lots of nice toys,' says Max. 'You should thank God for them.' So we do.

Let us be thankful and so worship God.
Hebrews 12:28

Max and I play on the swings. I feel sad because this is my last time at the play park. Max says, 'There will be another park at your new home. You should thank God for that.' So we do.

I say goodbye to my friends. This makes me feel sad. Max says, 'Thank God for the new friends you will make.' So we do.

I will give thanks to the Lord. Psalm 7:17

When we get home there is a van parked outside the house. Some men are carrying furniture out to the van. There is my mum's lamp, the mirror from the hall, the washing machine and my little bed.

I feel worried. Will the men give us our furniture back?

Max says, 'Of course they will. It's good you've got all that furniture - that's another thing to thank God for.' Max is good at this game.

Let the peace of Christ rule in your hearts ....
And be thankful. Colossians 3:15

I feel sad when I see the empty house. There are no pictures on the walls or curtains in the windows. Dad is giving the keys to the new owners.

From now on someone else will sleep in my room. Max says, 'You will have a brand new room, all to yourself.' I nod my head and say, 'Yes! I will thank God for that.'

Give thanks to the Lord for he is good.
Psalm 136:1

When it is time to go Max waves goodbye. He looks really sad. Then I remember something. 'You can come and stay with me soon, Max. So let's thank God for that!' Max smiles, Digger wags his tail and then we wave goodbye.

It's a long journey to our new home. As we drive past the play park, my old school, and the shops I thank God that he never changes. Jesus is the same always. I can always trust him.

Thanks be to God who always leads us.
2 Corinthians 2:14

When we arrive at our new house I see that our furniture has arrived safely. Our new home looks nice. There is a dog house for Digger and I will have a new bedroom all to myself.

I meet some other children who take me to the park down the road. I have made lots of new friends already. I feel really happy. I thank God for looking after me so well.

We give thanks to you, O God ...
for your Name is near. Psalm 75:1

When it is time to go to bed I count all the things that I have thanked God for. There are lots and lots. Mum helps me to write a postcard to Max to tell him all about our journey and my new home.

I tell Max that I hope he will come and see me soon. I thank God for my new home and my best friend Max.

You are my God and I will give thanks.
Psalm 118: 28

You can say thank you to God for your home:

Dear God,

Thank you for my home and for my family who live with me. Help us all to love you more. I want you to be the most important person in our home.

Thank you Jesus for leaving your special home in heaven to come to live in my world. Thank you that if I love you and trust in you, one day your home in heaven will be my home too.

Help me to believe in you and love you more each day.

Amen.